D1466889

Can You Find These
Trees?

Carmen Bredeson and
Lindsey Cousins

Enslow Elementary
an imprint of

Enslow Publishers, Inc.
40 Industrial Road
Box 398
Berkeley Heights, NJ 07922
USA

http://www.enslow.com

Enslow Elementary, an imprint of Enslow Publishers, Inc.
Enslow Elementary® is a registered trademark of Enslow Publishers, Inc.

Library of Congress Cataloging-in-Publication Data

Bredeson, Carmen.
  Can you find these trees? / Carmen Bredeson and Lindsey Cousins.
      p. cm. — (All about nature)
  Includes index.
  Summary: "Introduces pre-readers to simple concepts about trees using short sentences and
repetition of words"—Provided by publisher.
  ISBN 978-0-7660-3981-0
  1. Trees—Juvenile literature. 2. Trees—Identification—Juvenile literature. I. Cousins,
Lindsey. II. Title.
  QK475.8.B73 2012
  582.16—dc23   2011034143

Future editions:
Paperback ISBN: 978-1-4644-0070-4
ePUB ISBN 978-1-4645-0977-3
PDF ISBN 978-1-4646-0977-0

Printed in China
012012 Leo Paper Group, Heshan City, Guangdong, China
10 9 8 7 6 5 4 3 2 1

To Our Readers: We have done our best to make sure all Internet Addresses in this book
were active and appropriate when we went to press. However, the author and the publisher
have no control over and assume no liability for the material available on those Internet sites
or on other Web sites they may link to. Any comments or suggestions can be sent by e-mail
to comments@enslow.com or to the address on the back cover.

Photo Credits: © 2011 Photos.com, a division of Getty Images. All rights reserved., pp. 4, 6,
8, 20, 22, 23; Shutterstock.com, pp. 1, 3, 7, 9, 10, 11, 12, 13, 14, 15, 16, 17, 18, 19, 21

Cover Photo: Shutterstock.com

Note to Parents and Teachers

Help pre-readers get a jump-start on reading. These lively stories introduce simple concepts
with repetition of words and short simple sentences. Photos and illustrations fill the pages
with color and effectively enhance the text. Free Educator Guides are available for this
series at www.enslow.com. Search for the *All About Nature* series name.

Contents

Words to Know...................... 3
Trees 5
Oak 7
Maple 9
Pine 11
Ash................................... 13
Cottonwood 15
Weeping Willow 17
Paper Birch 19
Redbud 21
Holly 23
Learn More: Books and Web Sites .. 24
Index 24

Words to Know

acorn

pinecone

squirrel

3

Trees

Trees are used for many things.

Birds build nests in trees.

Apples grow on trees.

You can sit under a tree.

It is a good thing there are
many trees.

Can you find some of the trees
in this book?

5

Oak

acorn

Oak trees grow very tall.

They can grow wide, too.

Acorns grow on oak trees.

Squirrels eat acorns.

Deer, mice, and bears eat acorns, too.

Do you have acorns near your home?

7

Maple

Maple leaves

are shaped

like a hand.

The points spread

out like fingers.

Maple leaves turn many

colors in the fall.

They turn red, yellow, and orange.

Look for these colorful leaves in

the fall.

Pine

Pine leaves
are shaped
like needles.
The needles do not
fall off the tree in the winter.
The trees stay green all year.
Pine trees grow pinecones.
Some people use a pine tree for
their Christmas tree.

Ash

Look at a leaf

on an ash tree.

There are points on its sides.

They look like tiny teeth.

Ash trees have strong wood.

Baseball bats are made

of ash wood.

Look at a baseball bat.

Think about how it used to be

part of an ash tree.

Cottonwood

Cottonwood trees
have shiny leaves.
The leaves turn
yellow in the fall.

These trees make seeds
in the spring.
The seeds have fluff around them.
They look like cotton.
Do you think this is why it is called
a cottonwood tree?

Weeping Willow

Weeping willow leaves

are long and thin.

The branches

bend down.

Sometimes they even touch the ground.

Willow trees like water.

They grow best next to

rivers and ponds.

Look for a weeping willow the next

time you are near water.

17

Paper Birch

Paper birch trees are tall and thin.

The bark is white with black marks.

Birch trees grow close together.

They look like big white sticks.

Birch leaves turn yellow in the fall.

Redbud

The buds on a
redbud tree are
not red.

They are pink.

The buds bloom in the spring.

They bloom into pink flowers.

They cover the whole tree.

Have you ever seen a redbud tree?

Holly

Holly trees have
leaves with points.
They also have
red berries.

You should never eat the berries.

They can make you sick.

Holly leaves stay green all year long.

Holly trees grow in many places.

Bet you can find one if you look

really hard!

Read More

Hawk, Fran. *Count Down to Fall.* Mount Pleasant, S.C.:
Sylvan Dell Publishing, 2009.

Gibbons, Gail. *Tell Me, Tree: All About Trees for Kids.* Boston:
Little Brown Books for Young Readers, 2002.

Web Sites

Enchanted Learning. <http://www.enchantedlearning.com/themes/
trees.shtml>
Real Trees 4 Kids. <http://www.realtrees4kids.org>

Index

acorns, 7
ash, 13
baseball bat, 13
berries, 23
Christmas tree, 11
cottonwood, 15
fluff, 15

holly, 23
maple, 9
needles, 11
oak, 7
paper birch, 19
pine, 11
pinecones, 11

redbud, 21
water, 17
weeping willow, 17

Guided Reading Level: E
Guided Reading Leveling System is based on the guidelines
recommended by Fountas and Pinnell.

Word Count: 396